MOODS OF
CARDIGAN BAY

MOODS OF
CARDIGAN BAY

NICK JENKINS

HALSGROVE

First published in Great Britain in 2006

Copyright: text and photographs © 2006 Nick Jenkins

British Library Cataloguing-in-Publication Data
A CIP record for this title is available from the British Library

ISBN 1 84114 531 9
ISBN 978 1 84114 531 0

HALSGROVE
Halsgrove House
Lower Moor Way
Tiverton, Devon EX16 6SS
Tel: 01884 243242
Fax: 01884 243325
email: sales@halsgrove.com
website: www.halsgrove.com

Printed and bound by D'Auria Industrie Grafiche Spa, Italy

INTRODUCTION

Some years ago I was approached by a colleague who was keen to publish a book of my photographs covering Cardigan Bay. The idea bubbled under for a year or two, then disappeared completely. Meanwhile, I kept it in my pending tray, knowing that this stretch of the Welsh coast had such huge photographic potential it would quite probably come to the surface at some point in the future. The present volume confirms my belief.

Cardigan Bay is that long stretch of coastline of Wales which extends roughly from Fishguard to the Lleyn Peninsula. From the air, it looks like a large bite has been taken out of the the western coastline of Wales. The scenery is both varied and fascinating as it sweeps round the bay, ranging from flat, shingle beaches to high, majestic cliffs and including several very large river estuaries. And in between are to be found some of the prettiest towns in Wales.

Barmouth on the mouth of the River Mawddach is idyllically situated, sheltered from the incoming sea by a large sand bank. The railway bridge crossing the Mawddach Estuary is a well-known landmark. Aberdovey is also at the mouth of a river, this time the Dovey, and it stands beneath the hills to the north of the vast estuary. It has to be said that in between the many pretty little coves and inlets, there are probably more caravan sites here than most other coastlines in Britain. But all those caravaners merely reinforce the fact that Cardigan Bay must have something worth seeing. And it certainly has.

The coast of Cardigan Bay offered me every possible photographic opportunity a UK coastline has to offer. There are always inherent problems in photographing on the coast. Probably the worst is the ever-present risk of getting sand and or sea spray into the camera. This is not helped by the fierce winds which frequently strike this coastline. Another challenge, and one that certainly has far more impact on the final images, is that of the dreaded sloping horizon. Great care was taken to ensure that the horizons were all straight in the camera viewfinder. This was done by the use of a nifty little spirit level, mounted onto the top of the camera.

Challenges aside, however, I once again embarked on a voyage of discovery. As with my previous book, *Moods of Mid Wales,* I started to find places I had no idea existed. Ancient little churches were encountered, one of them, at Llandanwg, all but buried in encroaching sand dunes.

Much if not all of this book was photographed during sorties when I was on my own, and in a complete cross section of the infamously fickle UK weather. This ranged from lashing rain and a howling gale at Borth, to glorious summer sunshine at Llangrannog. This portfolio of shots is meant to accurately reflect the changing moods of an exposed and lengthy coastline and, in my view, would not succeed in showing those moods if every photograph was full of happy, smiley people in idyllic summer sunshine.

I had a wonderful experience both taking and selecting images which I feel truly represent the *Moods of Cardigan Bay*. I hope the book inspires you as much as it inspired me, and tempts you to go out and see for yourself what a wonderful and varied stretch of coastline exists in Cardigan Bay.

Nick Jenkins
April 2006

DEDICATION

To my wife Anne and son Stephen, who once more have put up with my enforced absences from home. Their support is greatly appreciated.

Sunset over Clarach Beach
As seen here, the skies over Cardigan Bay can produce stunning sunsets.

River Teifi at Cardigan
This peaceful final stretch of the river seems to be almost frozen in time.

River Teifi at Cardigan
A boat moored on the River Teifi at Cardigan.

River Teifi at Cardigan
The river was so calm on this day that all the moored boats were beautifully reflected in the water.

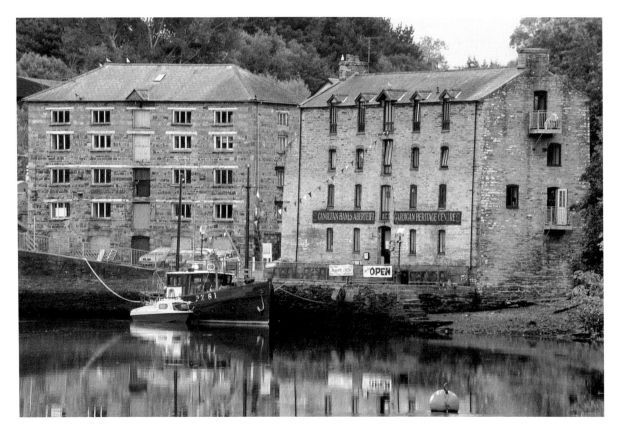

The old warehouses at Cardigan
These warehouses would have seen much activity when the River Teifi was the
main trade route in and out of Cardigan and the surrounding countryside.

Seafront at Aberystwyth
Photographed on a bitterly cold and very windy day.

Aberystwyth Royal Pier
Opened in 1865, the pier looks as solid today as the day it was built.

Aberystwyth Harbour
I loved the way the low winter sun tinged the fishermans' ropes with a honey yellow hue.

Aberystwyth Inner Harbour
It was the reflections in the water which caught my eye.

Aberystwyth Front
Tall and graceful, these buildings are mostly either guest houses or student accommodation.

Aberystwyth Front
The large building is part of the University of Wales, bought in 1874 to launch the university.

Aberystwyth Front
This view shows in the distance the well-known funicular railway climbing up the hillside just outside the town.

Morfa Bychan Beach at Porthmadog
This is a vast expanse of open sandy beach just north of Portmeirion.

Portmeirion

This 'designer' village on a peninsula on the Glaslyn estuary is the creation of the architect and evironmentalist Sir Clough Williams-Ellis. The whole village is designed as an Italianate dream and attracts many visitors. The picture shows the Campanile, or bell tower.

The Concrete Boat at Portmeirion

This 'trick' boat, permanently moored on the side of the vast Glaslyn Estuary, has fooled more folk than they might be prepared to admit.

Llangrannog
A small but, in season, very busy little coastal settlement, and home to the Urdd Wales Youth movement's summer camp.

Llangrannog Beach and Ynys Lochtyn
This spot is always popular with families in the summer, with its sandy beach and excellent coastal footpaths.

The Dyfi Estuary
Looking east up the River Dovey, or in Welsh, Dyfi.

Looking up the Dyfi Estuary from Ynyslas
I did not realise the vastness of the estuary until I came here to photograph it.

Aberdyfi and the Dyfi Estuary
This pretty seaside harbour town is just inside the Snowdonia National Park
and stands beneath the hills that run right down to the coast.

Aberdyfi
These lobster pots stacked on the wooden quay will soon be put to use out in the bay.

Aberdyfi across the Dyfi Estuary
A photograph taken on a very moody day; the sunlight just refused to break through the clouds,
which in a way helped to create the sombre atmosphere.

The large beach at Aberdyfi
The lifebuoy added a splash of colour to an otherwise deserted beach on a grey winter day.

Mawddach Estuary at Barmouth
Trawler moored alongside the Aberdyfi harbour wall, with the
Cambrian Coast Railway bridge in the background.

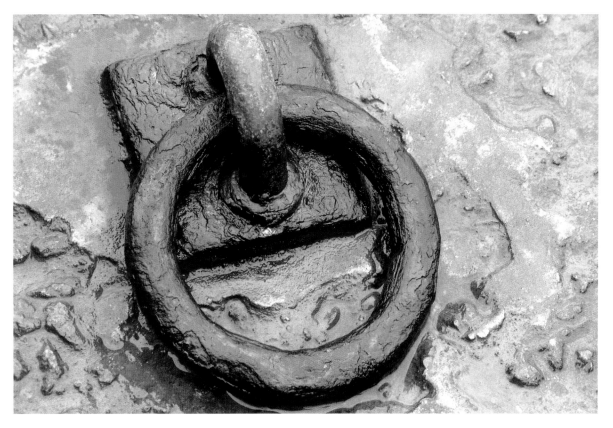

Barmouth harbour wall
Iron mooring ring, one of many, along the harbour wall at Barmouth.

Quayside at Aberdyfi
Pots and fisherman's rope at Aberdyfi quayside, emphasising the maritime nature of this little town.

Aberdyfi
Fishing boats brought up from the Dyfi Estuary for winter.

Penbryn Beach
Although only accessible by foot, the winding little path between the car park and the
beach builds up a sense of expectation, which is always fulfilled.

Penbryn Beach
This beach is a real delight for the coastline explorer.
An excellent little café stands in the middle of the nearby car park.

The seafront at Borth
The groynes were all that stood out on a windswept and rain-lashed beach.

Lochtyn Headland and Carreg Bica Rock *(centre)*
The rock is alleged to be one of the Devil's teeth which he ripped from his mouth and hurled
to the ground after suffering from the pain of a raging toothache.

The coastline near Cwm Tydu
I love this remote spot, especially late on a sunny summer evening when everything turns to a deep golden yellow.
The promontory in the middle ground is the site of Castell Bach, an Iron Age hillfort.

Castell Bach headland
This promontory, just north of Cwm Tydu Bay, is the site of an Iron Age hillfort,
its embankments clearly visible on the ground.

Above Castell Bach Beach
Fence above the beach at Castell Bach, near Cwm Tydu.
It caught my eye because it seemed to start and end nowhere.

Sunset on the cliffs near Cwm Tydu
I waited for over an hour to get this shot,
but was really pleased about the way the
sun struck the foreground rocks.

Cliff path at Cwm Tydu in high summer
The flowers just shone out,
backlit by the sun.

Contorted cliffs at Cwm Tydu
This is typical of the massive geological folding along this stretch of coastline.

Lone figure on Cwm Tydu Beach
This remote little cove becomes isolated in the winter, with only the very keen seeking it out.

The beach at Mwnt
Another of Cardigan Bay's many popular sandy beaches.

Coastline at Mwnt
Rugged and remote cliffs stand either side of the sandy beach and picturesque church.

The little church of the Holy Cross *(Eglwys y Grog)* **at Mwnt**
Sheltered from the gales of the Irish Sea by a rocky hillside, Mwnt was
believed to be a stopping-off point for pilgrims *en route* to St Davids.

Mwnt Church
Church bell at Mwnt.

Mwnt Church
The old rafters are still in superb condition.

Gravestone at Mwnt Church
Note that the epitaph is in Welsh,
which is often spoken in these parts.

Criccieth
The wide sweep of sand and pebbles of Criccieth Beach, beneath the imposing ruins of the thirteenth-century castle.

Harbour wall and boat at Criccieth
It is very common to see these little fishing boats brought up onto the beaches of Cardigan Bay.

Grey heron at Cardigan Nature Reserve
The heron did not move for about ten minutes, allowing me to take my time composing the photograph.

Cardigan Island from Gwbert on Sea
A popular spot not only because of the little farm zoo nearby but also for seal watching,
especially in the autumn when the seal pups begin to arrive.

Poppit Sands looking towards Cardigan Island
This huge expanse of sand just seems to swallow up anyone on it.

Poppit Sands
Looking south to the cliffs and rocks this popular beach presents a totally different perspective.

Porthmadog Harbour on the outflow of the Glaslyn River
This bustling little town is the starting point for the miniature railway line which runs up into the mountains and Blaenau Ffestiniog.

Porthmadog Harbour, Cwrt-y-Harbwr, the old harbour offices
Porthmadog was once a very busy port, chiefly for the export of slate from Snowdonia.

Porthmadog Harbour
Now a quiet tidal harbour for local craft, the harbour is a shadow of its former self. Recent works have made it possible to take an easy stroll along the old quayside and see what remains of the old harbour.

Porthmadog Harbour
These chains were once the means of securing the sloops and schooners which regularly berthed
here to carry away their cargos of slate to such far away locations as the USA.

Mawddach Estuary at Barmouth
View across the Mawddach River towards Cadair Idris.

Looking up the Mawddach Estuary towards Cadair Idris
The warmth of the winter morning light really lit up this landscape, especially with Cadair Idris topped with a white cap of snow.

Mawddach Estuary
A solitary fishing boat moored in the Mawddach Estuary at Barmouth.

Lobster pots at Barmouth
Cardigan Bay has many small towns which were once dependent on the harvest of the sea for their existence.

Toll bridge at Penmaenpool in the Mawddach Estuary
Still in private hands, this bridge provides a convenient short-cut across the estuary and the River Mawddach.

St Tanwg Church, Llandanwg
This little church is often buried in sand and frequently has to be dug out by local people.

Llandanwg Church
Headstone at Llandanwg Church, gradually being covered by the ever-encroaching sand dunes.

View to Y Llethyr from Llandanwg Beach
The wind was bitingly cold the day I took this picture. In fact, I was the only one to be seen for miles.

Llandanwg Beach looking north
The outline of Harlech Castle seen against the Snowdonia hills.

Harlech Castle
This imposing castle can be seen for miles up and down the coastline.
Many years ago the sea came right up to the base of the rocky crag on which it was built.

View towards the Lleyn Peninsula
This sweeping view across the northern section of Cardigan Bay shows well the
huge expanse of beach south of Harlech – as well as the size of the caravan sites.

Chimney pots in Harlech
I had just bought some sandwiches in the local shop when these smoking chimneys caught my eye.
They just said, 'a cold winter day in Harlech' to me.

Harlech
Hen Bethau, an antique shop in Harlech.

Snowdon from just outside Harlech
While not strictly Cardigan Bay, this view of Snowdonia's reigning peak
was taken from the flat marshes which surround Harlech.

Ceibwr Bay
On the Pembrokeshire Coastal Path, Ceibwr Bay is well known to walkers and naturalists alike.

**Ceibwr Bay, showing more detail
of the fascinating cliffs**
Geology students come here to study
the synclines and anticlines.

Cwm yr Eglwys Beach
The sandy cove offers excellent views across the water to Ceibwr Bay, along the high cliffs of the North Pembrokeshire coastline.

Cwm yr Eglwys
This secluded bay is dominated by the ruined remains of St Brynach's Church, all but demolished by heavy storms in 1859.
The light was superb when I last visited here, showing the church to best effect.

Rocks on Tresaith Beach
Wonderfully textured and a joy to photograph.

Rocks on Tresaith Beach… again
I took great pains to line up the grooves here.

Cliff at Tresaith Beach
I was fascinated by the totally different rock formations just across the beach.

Tresaith Beach
Many locals know this waterfall pouring
over the lip of the cliff.

Aberaeron Harbour
The Harbourmaster Hotel and houses in the outer harbour form part of one of the very first 'planned' towns in Wales.

Aberaeron Inner Harbour
Basking in the glow of a winter sun. For anyone who likes honey ice cream, it is very possible that they
will recognise the 'Honeypot on the Quay' shop on the left of the picture.

Aberaeron Outer Harbour
This busy little harbour is home to both fishing and pleasure boats.

Aberaeron Beach
A cold and windy day as the surf pounded the shingle. I should thank the two girls
who kindly shielded the sun off my camera lens for this shot.

Clarach Bay
The sun was just starting to set, giving these jagged rocks a dark and sombre outline.

Clarach Bay
A pebble is left behind as the tide recedes.

Clarach Bay
Kelp wilting in the falling tide.

Clarach Bay
A kelp stem still standing after the tide has gone out. It will soon topple over.

Coastline at Llansanffraid
A quiet little village near Llanrhystud.

Old beach hut at Llansanffraid
Needing some TLC, this hut was all the more photogenic for its seeming air of neglect.

St Bridget's Church, Llansanffraid
I was taken by the large purple-hued slates making up the walls of the church, something I had not seen before.

New Quay harbour wall
This very popular seaside resort is usually all but empty out of season.

New Quay *(Cei Newydd)*
The sandy north beach, protected by the harbour wall, fills up with visitors in the summer months.

New Quay
Boats tied along the north harbour wall. Despite its attraction as a holiday resort,
New Quay also relies on its fishing industry to earn an income.

New Quay
Boats taken out of the water for maintenance, before being put to sea for the fishing season.

New Quay
Lobster pots drying in the sun. Despite being a tourist town, New Quay also depends on fishing for its economic survival.

New Quay Harbour
New Quay from the main harbour wall or quay.

New Quay
Terraced houses run neatly along the hillside overlooking the rocky south beach.

St Dogmaels Abbey, North Pembrokeshire
Founded in 1115, the abbey, now in ruins and in the care of Cadw, always provides a peaceful haven from life's rush.

St Dogmaels
St Thomas's Church in St Dogmaels, next to the remains of the abbey.

Beach at Aberporth
The river cuts a large loop on its way to the sea.

Aberporth
Boat in the tiny 'harbour' of Aberporth.

Unloading the day's catch, Aberporth
Apparently many of the crabs and lobsters caught around this coastline are destined for the Spanish market.

Aberporth
This fisherman was happy to pose
for me with his lobsters.

Small boat and lobster pots, Aberporth
A typical sight on the Ceredigion coastline.

Aberporth
South Beach is separated from North Beach by a small headland.

The carved wooden dolphin above Aberporth South Beach
Dolphins are not an uncommon sight in Cardigan Bay, but I have yet to train my lens on them successfully.

Road sign on Newport Sands
I was fascinated to see such a sign in the middle of a deserted beach.

Newport Sands
I was attracted by the beautiful sheen of the winter sun reflected on the wet sand.

Newport Sands
A vast stretch of dark coloured sand with the Preseli Hills in the background.

Carn Ingli in the Preseli Hills
This shot was taken just before a sleet downpour.

Right: **The Nevern Celtic Cross**
Considered to be Romano British
in origin, the cross stands over
16 feet/5 metres high.

Below: **The Nevern Celtic Cross**
A detail, showing some of the
wonderfully intricate carvings.

Nevern
Mounting steps outside the church gate, thought to be one of only two surviving sets in Pembrokeshire.

Clapper bridge over the stream at Nevern
This serene spot is well known for its church and ancient stones.

The remains of the old iron furnace at Furnace
These splendid ruins are now in the care of Cadw and are sometimes called the Dyfi Furnace, which is the correct name in Welsh.

Old iron works, Furnace
Close up of the centre of the massive water wheel, used to drive the bellows in the old iron furnace.

Waterfall at Furnace
The falls are right beside the site of
the old furnace, latterly a sawmill
and now a visitor attraction.

Llangelynnin Church, dedicated to St Celynin
Look out for the horse bier inside the church, which was used to carry the bodies
of deceased parishioners to the church by strapping the handles to a horse.

Llangelynnin Church
The archway of the old porch of Llangelynnin Church.

Llangelynnin Church
A single bell, dated 1842, hangs
over the church porch.

Fairbourne
Graffiti decorates these anti-tank blocks left on the pebbles of Fairbourne Beach.

Fairbourne
Rope name on one of the beach huts at the southern end of Fairbourne Beach.

Tonfanau Seafront
A very bleak day at Tonfanau, but there are still some intrepid water sports enthusiasts.

Tonfanau Railway Station
Old ticket office at Tonfanau Station on the Cambrian Coast Railway. I almost missed
this quaint little office, which was half-buried in undergrowth.

Broad Water, Towyn
Behind Towyn this large expanse of water is surrounded by reed beds. The marshes here once covered a vast area,
but land reclamation during the Victorian era has allowed much of the land to be used for farming.

Reed heads on Broad Water
Close up of reed heads on Broad Water.

Old Milestone on the A496
These old signs seem to be
getting rarer all the time.

Old Llanbedr Station
The station is now a private house, but this intriguing plaque has been left attached on the wall.

Looking up to Diffwys from Morfa Dyffryn Beach
This huge peak, the highest in the Rhinog Mountains, was lit up like a beacon every time the sun emerged from behind a cloud.

Morfa Dyffryn Beach
The low winter sun gave the surrounding dunes and wooden path decking a gorgeous golden hue.

View north along Morfa Dyffryn Beach
The size of the beach is immense, and the red pole added just a splash of colour to enhance the scene.

View south along Morfa Dyffryn Beach
Photographing into the sun gave me the lovely reflections on the wet sand.
This is the most enormous stretch of sand I can ever remember photographing.

Dyffryn burial chamber
This Neolithic burial chamber is reckoned to have been constructed between 3000 and 1000BC.
It is just a short walk off the road in the village of Dyffryn Ardudwy.

One of the two Dyffryn burial chambers
These chambers would have been buried in earth and stones, unlike today.
Local farmers saw these huge mounds of stone as a cheap and easy quarry.

Shell Island Causeway
This solitary wooden hut looked to be so out of place in this huge, sandy landscape.

From Shell Island Causeway to the Rhinogs
The sun lit these snow-capped mountains like beacons.

Pwll Gwaelod
This beautiful and remote cove is just a stone's throw away from the busy ferry terminal at Goodwick,
but might as well be one hundred miles away for its feeling of tranquillity.

Cliffs at Pwll Gwaelod
The cliffs here are a mix of water-washed rocks
and jagged slaty edges. The colours in the slates
are wonderfully varied.

Old Abergwaun

This charming little fishing village lies sheltered by the surrounding hills. The film of Dylan Thomas's epic poem,
Under Milk Wood was made here, and starred Richard Burton, Elizabeth Taylor and Peter O'Toole.

Old Abergwaun
Sometimes referred to as Lower Fishguard,
this seaside village always offers superb
subjects to photograph.

Old Abergwaun Harbour
The fact that the tide was out meant that the yachts and fishing boats were all keeled over at interesting angles.

Old Abergwaun Harbour
Fishing is still active here, as is borne out by these beached trawlers.

Old Fort, Fishguard

Now maintained by the Pembrokeshire Coast National Park, the fort was built around 1780 following a bombardment of Fishguard by pirates. The last firing of the cannons was in 1797 when the last invasion of Britain, by a small contingent of French sailors, took place at nearby Carreg Gwastad Point.